Say
What
You
Mean

Say
What
You
Mean

*How To Attract Woman and Maintain
The Relationship*

John Beauvais

Say What You Mean

Legal & Disclaimer

The information contained in this book and its contents is not designed to replace or take the place of any form of medical or professional advice; and is not meant to replace the need for independent medical, financial, legal, or other professional advice or services, as may be required. The content and information in this book have been provided for educational and entertainment purposes only.

The content and information contained in this book have been compiled from sources deemed reliable, and it is accurate to the best of the Author's knowledge, information, and belief. However, the author cannot guarantee its accuracy and validity and cannot be held liable for any errors and/or omissions. Further, changes are periodically made to this book as and when needed. Where appropriate and/or necessary, you must consult a professional (including but not limited to your doctor, attorney, financial advisor, or such other professional advisor) before using any of the suggested remedies, techniques, or information in this book.

Upon using the contents and information contained in this book, you agree to hold harmless the Author from and against any damages, costs, and expenses, including any

The Beginning

Seven point four billion people in the world, and yet you are still single. Do you often ask yourself why you are single? Do you find yourself in awe of people in relationships and think, how did they have it so easy? Do you regularly look in the mirror or daydream about why you cannot seem to find a partner? Do you speculate almost every other day (or every day, who are we kidding here!) if you will die alone? (Hmm, a scary prospect indeed.) Do you sigh sadly, all alone on those nights meant to be for cuddling, or those days perfect for long drives? Are you extremely agitated because I am just pinching your wounds right now, and I should stop?

Is that an exasperated yes as you pause and wonder if you want to read on further? I strongly suggest you do.

This book is an instruction manual, a giver of tips of dos and don'ts to help you get the person you ultimately deserve, the one who is right for you.

Table of Contents

Read the book, pause and take in the knowledge and then apply it to increase your chances of decreasing those single lonely nights.

Introduction

"It is our choices, Harry, that show what we truly are, far more than our abilities."
~ **J.K. Rowling**

The choices we make have a profound influence on our lives. Our choices control our present and affect our future life too. We hold tremendous power inside us, and through our choices, we can use that power. For example, the moment Rosa Parks refused to give up her seat, she unleashed the power within her. It was her choice to stand against racial discrimination, and by wielding it, she changed the course of history. We can cite many such incidents where our choices have left a deep impact on our lives.

Our choices show who we are; they test our abilities and help us to surpass all obstacles. The choices make us face challenges and emerge victorious. They empower us to try tough goals, and as we achieve more, our confidence soars.

So, think and make a choice in every situation of your life. We cannot control what happens to us, but we can control how we react to situations. So, wield your power, make a choice and stand by it.

Do you know what sets us apart from other species on this earth? It is the power of words.

> "Words and magic are two powerful forces that can change the world."
> ~ **Amy Neftzger**

Words give us a perpetual flow of creativity. Through words, we can express our intent, connect to others, and create a bond that transcends time and space.

Our words can be a soothing balm on someone's wound, or we can use them to ignite passion. Our words can light someone's dreams; they can give someone another reason to live. If we want, we can use words to heal or hurt others. It all depends on how we choose to use them. People with good intent use words to benefit others. They use words to manifest their dreams, for the word is a magnificent tool to change this world. Think of Nelson Mandela, Martin Luther King, and Gandhi. How they inspired millions of people and changed their lives.

On the other hand, people with bad intentions or people full of spite use their words to bring destruction. They use this power to demean others.

So, make a choice today. Use your words to live the life of your dreams, rise to the occasion and fight for yourself and others. Use these supreme powers God has bestowed upon you to create a beautiful life.

Chapter 1

Self-Awareness and Motivation

"Anyone who has never made a mistake has never tried anything new."
–Albert Einstein

D o you know what commands respect? Why are some people revered always? Because of their words. Yes, what we say defines our character, and people who stand by their words command respect from others. Other characteristics make a person great but valuing your words and being honest is the most vital.

Stand by your words
A man who means what he says will always be respected by his fellowmen. To stand out in a crowd, you have to show integrity, and choosing your words carefully, is the first step towards being a man of integrity.

We need to be perfect with our words. By faultless or impeccable, we mean our words should not go against ourselves. They should be honest and express our intention. You should always mean what you say. If you promise anything, please deliver it. By being true to your words, you will gain confidence. People will always look up to you, and reaching your goals will become easier.

Be impersonal to criticism

As you embark on your self-development journey, people may criticize you. It is natural to face flak from those who don't understand your ordeal. If you take those opinions seriously, you will never progress in life. So, be impersonal and pay attention to your goals in life. If you keep listening to others and change your course based on their views, you will face hurt and disappointment. However, if you don't take the comments personally, you will feel positive and experience joy. So, be impersonal to others and listen only to your heart.

Have open communication

We have mentioned earlier that only humans are bestowed with the power of words, and the ability to express our feelings and thoughts sets us apart from other animals on this planet. We must establish free and open communication channels with people around us. Most of the time, we assume what others are thinking and make decisions based on our assumptions. It creates tension in a relationship. So, stop presuming and start asking questions. You will get clear answers that will help you to understand others better.

When people ask you anything, give truthful answers. Yes, when you say what you mean, you come out as an honest person whom people can rely upon. It forges strong relationships.

Do your best

What is the secret behind the success of Michael Phelps? His hard work and dedication. Whether an athlete, world leader, or writer, if you study their lives, you will find one common factor – they gave their best to their job. Yes, doing your best is the key to success.

If you have a target in life, dedicate your mind to achieving it. However, don't judge yourself if you fail. Try again; giving your best is your duty. Moreover, don't forget the previous three lessons. You have to be true to yourself, be honest with your words, and never assume anything about anyone.

By following these four principles diligently, you can lead a happy life. You will experience abundance and attain any goal you have set for yourself. You may ask that if tasting success is so simple, why doesn't everyone succeed? Why do we find only a handful of people reaching their goals? What stops the majority of people from realizing their dreams?

The answer lies in our internal beliefs.

What makes success so difficult to attain?

When we were born, we were free. We were free to think and act. If you observe a child, you will know what spontaneity means. As we grow older, we pick up social rules from our environment and society. We are forbidden to express our desires and feelings. We are forced to follow social rules;this conditioning makes us forget our true selves. We try to be like others; we give up originality.

Isn't this harmful? Yes, but how many of us realize this? We are unaware of our true selves and potential. We continue to follow the meaningless rules that rob us of happiness.

It is time to wake up from our slumber. It is time to realize who we are. If you are honest with yourself, you know what motivates you, and if you are aware of your objective, life will be simpler.

So, start listening to your heart. Meditate and spend some time every day in contemplation. It will help you to connect to your inner self. You will also know your true calling. Once you know this, all you have to do is to follow the four rules and find success and happiness in life.

On this journey of self-discovery, you will come to know the beliefs that hinder your growth. Replace them with good ones. Forget the conditioning that society imposed on you. It is time to break the shackles.

Whenever someone does anything negative or harmful, don't fret over it. It is their action; they are responsible for it. Your true self should not be bothered by others' actions. Don't entangle yourself in the negative emotions of others.

"Forgiveness is the fragrance that the violet sheds on the heel that has crushed it."
~ Mark Twain

Forgiveness is power. It is the power to forget and carry on your path. It is the power to stand apart, say no to negative feelings, and embrace goodness. People who practice forgiveness attain peace of mind. They remain calm and composed even when life gets unfair. They are not moved by others' follies nor by mishaps.

So, start practicing forgiveness. Begin with yourself. Yes, forgive your negative thoughts; pardon your failure. Rise again if you have faltered, and keep following your path.

Life becomes beautiful when you simplify it. Consider each day as a gift and spend it wisely. Like everybody else, you have limited time and so use it properly.

Regain your personal power and spend it on positive things. Use this force to bring great changes.

So, now you know how you can be what you were meant to be. You have to find the source of your inner power and tap it whenever life demands it. Read along to know how you can discover this fountain of motivation and power and taste success in your endeavors.

Chapter 2

What Mistakes Are You Making?

"Character consists of what you do on the third and fourth tries."
- James A. Michener.

Remember, "Winners never quit, and quitters never win." As just like any other life endeavor, attracting and dating beautiful women is not going to happen to you with a snap of fingers.

My mother once told me, "Because of yourself," the first time I screamed out to myself, "Why not me?". "DAMN," was her chilly, cutting words.

On one hand, I had to face the hardfacts of life. When we're chasing things we enjoy or love, we tend to get carried away too quickly, which is when things go south. Realizing our very own faults and working on them helps us appear less 'desperate' when people see us in tough situations. Keeping an eye out for things we might be doing incorrectly will help us fix them, and help us stay in control always.

"The sea is teeming with fish." That's something you have probably heard before, didn't you? To begin, I'd want to point out some of the reasons why it's so difficult for you to meet your much-desired 'soulmates'.

I've seen men stare blankly at women as if they anticipate something out-of-the-blue to happen. I've also seen who are a little too forward. When they publicly hit on a woman in a bar, they "magically" expect that she will instantly fall in love with them.

Obviously surprised, they ask, "Why can't I find someone?" Finding a companion isn't that simple, especially in this day and age when dating apps like Tinder are widely available and used by singles.

Now that I've brought up Tinder allow me to provide some advice on how to properly approach women on the dating app. There is no doubt that Tinder, a popular dating app, has made finding a companion easier for men in the online dating scene. There's more to the approach than just signing on, swiping, and waiting for the "magic" to happen.

How Can You Effectively Talk to Women on Tinder?
Just like Sir Edmund Hillary rightly said: *"It is not the mountain we conquer, but ourselves."* Guys who haven't

been on a date in months commonly believe, "It's a waste of time to meet people on the internet".

There is no way we can blame the entire chicken industry for a terrible chicken leg at KFC.If we can't find love online, and the same is true when it comes to finding love offline,there is only one guy to blame, and that is "you".

Tinder is the best dating app in, well, ever. My friends and I had never gone on so many dates in such a short period with so little effort. The best thing about Tinder is that it lets you "speed date." You match with a girl, have a little banter back and forth, and you have a date. Yes, not every female will agree to a romantic evening under the stars, but they are on Tinder for a purpose, and if they have swiped right on you, they have already considered meeting you. With that said, let me walk you through Tinder's golden rules so you may reap the same rewards that so many other men have.

Also, remember, one thing to keep in mind is that women are constantly browsing through their texts. If you want your message to be noticed, it must be original and distinct from the competition. It must arouse her interest and hold her gaze. So, your first sentence cannot be a simple "Hello". That will not work, buddy.

When it comes to using dating apps, most people pretend to be someone they're not. Bloviating and self-promotion will not automatically elevate your status. Some women view this conduct as childish and obsessive. It's possible to subtly highlight positive aspects of your personality. Instead of "I've gone to many locations because I'm wealthy enough," you may write, "I love how beautiful the globe is, and I'm so happy for being able to observe it with my own eyes" to describe how much you've traveled.

One more piece of advice is to say what you mean when you speak. Saying you've been in love (when you haven't) or are the right guy for her (when you're not) will make you appear ungrounded and uninterested. When conversing, use etiquette and fluidity to your advantage. Having an adult conversation with a female and letting her judge your personality will demonstrate your maturity. The goal is not to be **overbearing or clingy**.

Conversation Starters

Okay, you should instantly forget *your* never-ending line of "What's up, how are you?" NEVER use that line again!!!

Do you have any idea how many dates a gorgeous woman may get in a day? And you keep opening with that uninteresting, trite, and uninspiring line. For real?

For the time being, imagine yourself in the position of a female. She has already signed up for a Tinder account.

Most likely as a result of her being bored and curious. The only way to get through to these girls is to make it fun.

Here are a few of my personal favorites:

My first message
1. *I got a question?*

Second follow-up message
1. Why girl like yourself still single?

IF she seems not sure why she is single, hit her with "Are you a crazy type?"

Third follow-up message
1. What are you looking for on Tinder?

Her answer will show you which directions you could take

Random Question
1. How's Tinder been treating you so far? Scary or fun-filled?
2. *Don't forget about me.*
3. What funny excuse have you given to leave a party early?
4. Any magical power you wish you had?

5. Is our anniversary when we first matched or when we first texted lol?

(This message shows her that you have confidence, she thinks you already got her but you really do)

Remember: You should ask these questions or similar ones which require a response purely the way you have asked them. Also, all of these questions highlighted above, I have personally used them on around a hundred girls, and guess what, I get an average of 85% response rate.

I know it's simple but really effective in the messaging game, but **women love mystery**, so base most of your questions *mysteriously* and creatively. You could also easily start with "I've got a question for you." Then after she responds, you could follow up on any of the options above.

Lastly, remember, no one wants to read an essay. So, keep it as short as possible: one or two sentences long.

When To Double Text

For many people, the first few weeks of texting a new crush can be nerve-racking, probably because of how stigmatized texting several times has become. In the world of modern dating, double-texting or messaging someone twice or more in a row is a passionately discussed topic. Some worried guys are concerned about how many messages are too many in succession since they don't want to appear needy or bothersome.

Despite its terrible reputation, there is no hard and fast rule when it comes to double-texting. As with everything in relationships or creating a connection with another person, there really shouldn't be any too broad right or wrong standards. Regarding whether it's acceptable to double text your crush, I would say, depending on the situation and substance, sure!

Well, let's take a look at some of these scenarios of double texting after a long silence period/no replies:

1. You: "Are you still alive?" *(Use the skull emoji at the end)* 💀
2. You: Change of plan - dinner is at 7 and the movie at 8.30.

This text shows her that you got her, and she is willing to go out with you.

This text also works on girls you didn't talk to in months. But make sure you sent out this text at 5:00 o'clock (set a reminder on your phone, lol).

Basically, she is going to text you back – wrong person. Then you'll text her back, "Sorry, how have you been?"

(If she texts you back, reply to her once between 7 to 8:30 hour).

3. You: I guess I take my joke back. Lol.
4. You: "Did you faint after receiving that last text from me? It happens. So, what else is new?"
5. You: "Your responses are too fast for me. Slow down, speedy.
6. You: "Hey there! Haven't heard from you in a while. Got kidnapped by E.T. and his pals or something?"
7. You: "If you go to jail, I'm the guy that could break you out.

Remember: If you start to feel bad, put down your phone and let the other person respond at their own pace. Double-texting is not inherently negative or detrimental to one's self-esteem. However, keep an eye out for obsessive thoughts about double-texting.

If you find yourself checking your messages obsessively every few minutes or seconds, feeling anxious about not receiving a response promptly, or feeling overburdened by the discussions itself, it may be time to put the phone down.

Golden Rule
Some men believe it is impossible to find the love of your life on Tinder. But it's possible she's looking for someone just like you. I was matched with a female on

Tinder, and she was surprisingly everything I wanted in a girl. She's brilliant, cute, witty, a gym junkie, down-to-earth, and so much more. When I first met her, I never considered making her my girlfriend since I assumed I'd end up with someone like Rihanna.(shout out to ASAP Rocky for getting Rihanna pregnant, I'd be lying if I never thought I would make her pregnant, but anyways.)

Don't misunderstand me. The girl I'm referring to was a dime a dozen, but I wanted someone famous. Stupid me; I had someone who complimented me while treating her as if she weren't significant enough for me. She was one of my greatest blessings, and now she treats me as if we never met! That is why, as I previously stated, you must understand why you are entering into a relationship. You must find it within yourself, or you will be bound to failed relationships for the rest of your life.

Tinder and other similar apps benefit both men and women. With a simple swipe on their mobile phones, even persons of the same gender limit or filter out the people they want to date. They judge and react without the inconvenience of meeting the individual first and not knowing what they look like, like in the old-school meet-up.

But have you ever considered whether you find someone who will perfectly fit into all of your needs (not just the attributes that you need, but also those that you merely desire) in one person? Can you locate the perfect person by filtering folks on your device's screen?

What Mistakes Are You Making?

Are you making any mistakes on dating apps? Why aren't you getting responses from anyone? Here is a list of common mistakes people generally make.

1. Having A Poor or Non-Existent Bio

I understand how difficult it is to write a dating app bio. You must condense your desirability into fewer than 500 words, striking a balance between being overly brief and waffling on endlessly about yourself. So, it's no surprise that so many men leave the "about you" area blank or write it with hackneyed one-liners ("If you don't look like your images, you're buying the drinks until you do," for example).

A strong bio, on the other hand, can be the difference between a left or right swipe, therefore you should definitely have one. Aim for one to three words that sum up your best qualities and explain what you're searching for in a woman in the funniest and most insightful way you can muster.

FUN FACT- Adding that you want to save the earth, you'll get more matches - (psychology thing).

2. Being Overly Picky

On the opposite end of the spectrum are the males who are naively swiping right like there's no tomorrow are the guys who are too picky about possible dates. These are the guys that swipe as if they're hard-to-please modeling scouts, with biographies that read like demanding wish lists of feminine traits, such as "You should be physically healthy, intelligent, and able to have a conversation."

"There will be no dog filters or mirror selfies. Redheads are my favorite." The woman of your dreams might find the dog filter amusing, so avoid being too specific in your search for dates and keep your mind and possibilities open.

Quick one: Let me share the story of a man who continually finds himself jumping from one relationship to another.

If you ask him how many relationships he has so far, you will only bore yourself to death waiting for him to tell you the stories of all the women he has been with. He started to date at age 16 and since then loved the idea of finding the "perfect girl" through the dating process and the fool-proof method of "try and try until you succeed".

One is too smart, the other too sensitive. The next one became too fat, the next one anorexic, and this countless list of complaints goes on. Years later,when he met his high school friends, most of them were already married with kids.

He started wondering why he couldn't secure a stable relationship and make a family of his own. He is a decent man with a high-paying job and stable career and surely can settle down with any lady he may choose. However, with all the unsuccessful past relationships that he has had, he can't seem to pull off the dating game again.

Take this man's story as a guide not to expect every good quality from one woman. As you are not perfect, every lady you may meet isn't a perfect machine that will serve all your needs too. Everybody has to compromise. But what we usually don't understand is every compromise isn't bad. When two people are willing to look over their flaws and create a harmonious relationship based on focusing on the good aspects, only then they can be truly happy and satisfied. We never know how many people are compromising with us, so it wouldn't hurt to compromise with them as well.

As obvious as this sounds, you will go nowhere with this perception of finding the perfect one because there is a high chance this person might not exist *(unless you know someone called Megan Fox, but we still do not know what her personality is like).*

3. Not Sure When To Call It A Day

Every woman has a story about losing interest in a guy on Tinder, only to have her inbox fill up with useless attempts to re-start the conversation, and then another, and another, and, my God, another, even after she's stopped responding.

Pleading a succession of "hey!" into the vacuum will not change her mind, so if your match has ceased responding to you, gracefully move on. You might have thought the chat was going well, or you might be bewildered that she's suddenly ghosted you, but that's part of dating, and there's nothing you can do about it except move on to the next, more passionate match. Don't squander anymore of your time.

It's easy to commit these blunders, and you may feel guilty or embarrassed about some of them. But don't worry too much; fortunately, each one has an easy cure, and now that you're aware of them, you can be confident that you'll be putting your best foot forward the next time you start swiping. Avoid these typical blunders, and you'll be racking up the matches and dates in no time.

Chapter 3

What Do You Want?

"When what you value and dream about doesn't match the life you are living, you have pain."
– Shannon L. Alder

D o you know why we feel frustrated with life? What makes us so unhappy? We do things that others tell us are important and ignore our own needs. Most of the time, you will find yourself following others without listening to your inner voice. In relationships, the qualities we seek in our partners also are governed by others.So, we remain unhappy in our relationships or fall for the wrong person. To find happiness in life, we have to prioritize our needs. We may want a lot of things in our partners, but how many of them are really important to us? What are the characteristics we cannot compromise with?

Set Priorities

Think of the qualities you need in your partner and rank accordingly. Think of the qualities you absolutely cannot compromise on, say positive character. Try to forget the qualities relatively lower in the ranking when you find someone with that character, like big eyes. Or if you need a partner who should have a good body, then forget their characteristics such as anger issues.

It is not unlikely that when you prioritize, you will find it easier to let go of the bad qualities. For example, you might fall for someone too well-spoken and eventually find their less curvy body attractive. It has happened. But here is the trick, prioritize sensibly. This comes with knowing **yourself.** Often men think they like one quality more than anything, but they are not being true to themselves and later on,end up hurting someone else. This also includes placing too much importance on physical appearance. You might argue that this is an innate feature in men, but this causes problems.

The qualities that you may find that your future partner should and should not have been called your non-negotiables. These will guide your dating game process and rule out persons in the first place that will never be effective as your long-term partner.

My friend Chris, an active member of the Church, had his set of non-negotiable qualities that he wanted in a potential life partner. According to his list, he wanted his life lady to be an active member of the Church, intelligent, open-minded, and belong to a decent family. You can see that his list did not include any physical attributes, which allows him to broaden his search for the perfect life partner. However, his specific requirements limit his options and the area of his search. Now, speaking, where do you think hecan find this girl? In a bar? Of course, it will be easier for him to find a girl inside the Church itself. Similarly, a guy who is into fitness and wants his life partner to be physically fit will most likely find her at a gym or any other sporting place. He is least likely to find her at a McDonald's at 2 pm on a Monday. When making your list of non-negotiable qualities, make sure to go as deep as you can. Often, we only think about surface-level qualities and end up feeling disappointed when we get to know the other person on a deeper level.

However, you should also cover all known qualities as they play a crucial role in finding your perfect partner when dating. The remaining characteristics you may not include in the list are those you can and should **compromise** if possible. These include some physical attributes that would not affect your romantic relationship.

Negative attitudes or qualities that may affect your relationship that were excluded from your non-negotiable list should be worked on later by both of you. It takes two to tango, so as they say.

It would be best to find someone who understands that physical appearance is not everything. And if still, you think physical appearance matters most, then rank the physical attributes like grading dimples number one and placing lesser importance on the rest.

Setting Unrealistic Expectations

Another reason which makes it hard to find someone is unrealistic expectations. "I will look at her, she will look perfect, will respond to me, and there will be an instant attraction between us." No, sorry." If you feel that your chemistry needs to be fireworks immediately, please, these are not the movies. There are those rare times when you click with one person instantly, you see her, you look at her, she responds with a smile, and you approach her, and things tick immediately.

However, these cases are rare, and most women are hesitant to move even in this day and age. You need to realize and accept that it takes time for people to open up and bond with another person. Not only that, sometimes people do not even like you in the first meeting. However, when they spend more time with you, they get to know you better and start to fancy you. It is okay if your chemistry is a bit off the first time you meet. Instead of trying to push the connection, you need to wait for the other person to open up or give it a second try at bonding. Do not disregard her if she did not have the prettiest smile in the room that moved you a little or if she was not curvy enough to arouse you every time; that girl might be more compatible with you than you could have imagined.

> "The best and most beautiful things in the world cannot be seen or even touched. They must be felt with the heart."
> – Helen Keller

Furthermore, you are facing difficulties because you are not looking for someone in the right place. If you think you can find a girl just at a party or a bar, then you are wrong (you are not Ryan Gosling, man). True, women look for men to communicate with at bars and parties, but the competition here tends to be too high, and there is a higher chance the woman will think you are not that serious. This depends on your priorities, too, though. For example, if you tend to find women who party attractive, maybe a party is the perfect setting.

Prioritizing should automatically help you learn where to look for someone who will interest you. For example, if you are into intellectual women, try going to the library and perhaps socializing over books. This will not only help you find someone according to your interests, but increase the surprise factor (about the surprise factor if you bond with a lady in a bar), and women love surprises. If you want your partner to be sporty, join a sports club and try to talk to someone about your favorite sport or, better yet, hear her talk about her passion for sports, and you might fall in love right there and then.

Communication

Communicationis extremely vital. Do you ever get astounded by just looking at the player who you know is a jerk and is still surrounded by women all the time? What is with him, you ask. This reminds me of that famous quote in the movie Perks of being the wallflower, "Why do I and everyone I love pick people who treat us like we're nothing." *Most of it is just communication which requires confidence. I know you look at a woman* you find attractive, and even the idea of talking to her makes you anxious.

You areprobably havingan anxiety attack but remember **THE FIRST STEP IS THE WORST**, and it gets more accessible from there onwards. Take a few confident steps towards her and say hi or just smile or even say something intense that might get you The attention you need.Remember what you wish for by staring at her butt. It's not that easy, you say; well, remember the preparation advice I gave in the beginning? Act upon it if you have some serious troubles with communication and familiarise yourself as the kid who always shook when he had to stand in front of the class. Try to stop the fear of rejection; according to famous author De Angelo try going to a mall and talking to every girl you see; this practice will make you understand how to naturally make a conversation with women.If you are still in college, this is the perfect time to learn this. Alongside that, learn how to make eye contact. (This is not about making eye contact when you are caught staring at her.)

These are some excellent tips that will remind you to stop overthinking.

1. Use the 5-second rule to make a decision within 5 seconds and spare yourself all the overthinking.
2. Don't indulge yourself in negative thoughts because when you do, it can be hard to stop. Your brain functions like a car without breaks going down a hill. So when you start thinking negative thoughts jump up out of the car.
3. Think that you are leading a group of people through a mission, and they are counting on you to make it through.
4. It might sound weird but think of your feet. It will stop your negative train of thoughts by diverting your attention from overthinking.
5. Think in the now because you can't change the past and know the future.

As you will learn later, ignorance and arrogance are a few of the top qualities women dislike in men. Furthermore, women tend to enjoy intense eye contact.

Sure, she might look away, but you should hold her gaze and see how she blushes. Don't worry if you feel shy at the moment. Use that shyness to seem mysterious.

If you still cannot help your shyness, turn that into a mystery. Women **love a mysterious guy**. Mold yourself so that your flaws appear as your assets.

Your Sense Of Style

Before we talk about your sense of style and how it has become a hurdle in love life, note that women love men who smell good. What does it mean by good? Women love an earthy and strong cologne on men. However, your cologne should not be so strong that it gets hard for them to breathe. They should think about your cologne in an arousing way and not how they wish the date would end so they could breathe properly.

Look, I am not here to judge your clothes or suggest what you should wear, but please guys, dressing style is important. I have a truck driver friend, 6ft 4 inches and big built. He scores every single time he is out just because of the way he dresses. He is more into casual dating, but he tells me his clean and smart dressing does the trick as women are impressed by his dress code and, of course, his charming personality.

Okay, back to you. The way you walk, talk or carry yourself, and your body language all play a huge role here. For example, if you are indeed color blind and wear a blue blazer with Willy-Wonka purple pants or any such absurd color combination, there is an issue. If your underwear still shows, there is an issue. If you wear clothes three sizes too small, there is an issue. If your smelly shirt has not been washed, and you can see stains on it, but you hope they won't be noticeable to others, there is an issue. If you are always fidgeting, some women might not appreciate that, or if your hand movements are awkward, that might be a turn-off. Honestly, these senses should not be that hard to know. Act **normal** and be presentable, and you will be in control of yourself and your body language.

Financial Stability

The next reason that most men complain about and think decreases the chances of finding a partner to zero is financial stability. Yes, women tend to place lots of importance on this; whether her partner can provide her with security. This has been linked to evolution, in the sense that women choose the best man possible, who can provide security, not just for her but for their children. This is important to understand. Even though we say that women like men to have something or the other, it does not necessarily have to mean that the guy must be wealthy. It means a man must strive to give his best in whatever he is doing. An excellent and comfortable life with someone loving and caring is preferable to an extremely lavish life without any love.

1. Read: Books provide you with the power to discover new skills and break out of ruts in your job.
2. Invest in Stocks: Get yourself a business coach and start investing!
3. Create multiple sources of income: We can no longer meet our bills with a single job or revenue stream.
4. Create personal boundaries and respect them: Mental boundaries are essential because you never want to be a kiss-ass.
5. Keep learning: Each of us will have periods in our careers when we aren't as busy as we would want, and this is the ideal time to continue learning.
6. Take a break: A weekend getaway is an excellent method to re-energize and rejuvenate yourself.
7. Start saving: It's amazing what a few bucks can do when added up for a month.

However, guys, times are genuinely changing women are continuing to earn more and more for themselves, and this lifts a lot of burden off the man (which reminds me; being a feminist will not only help women, it will help you too, and also women tend to be attracted to feminists, but of course, this does not imply that you should pretend to be a feminist when you are just a chauvinist.

If you are indeed in a situation of financial instability then do not thinkthat your game is over, women have been constructed to be more materialistic than they are.

There are things that genuinely matter more to women than money.

According to relationship coach Jordan Gray who surveyed women to find out what mattered more to women than money or cars, he found out the following characteristics:

- Drive (knowing what you want to be)
- Attention
- Your presence; being present
- Humour (been saving those jokes, now is the time to put them to good use)
- Being spontaneous
- Leadership

You **Will Learn** more about what women prefer in men later in the book.

For now, know that you still have the game even if you are broke. If you cannot pay the bill of that Sushi place, she likes then be creative and do something that costs less but means more like, as clichéd as this sounds, watching the sunset with popcorn, perhaps? Or perhaps cook for her and impress her with your culinary genius. Even if you can cook noodles, serve them on a beautiful plate, a garnish to two. Just be **sincere and honest**, and she will see and experience that.

Or express your vulnerability, and she might end up being attracted to you more. And of course, you expected me to say this, and I will say it, do everything you can to improve your situation. Take that job that pays less than you want it to pay, start writing for that consultancy, check the newspaper or do anything in your power.

Another thing to keep in mind is something that most people tend to ignore. While all the things mentioned above are crucial, we must remember that not everyone and everything is as shallow and materialistic as that. Women like a man who is passionate about more than just her.

A Hobby
A passion for a hobby or a cause can show a woman what you value in life and what a good person you are. A genuine man has his heart set on something other than just another human being. Be it a social or environmental cause or just a hobby that excites you, a woman will love to see that sparkle in your eyes when you talk about it. She will look at you as more than just a sexual partner. She will start to see you as someone she can spend her life with. You will be more humanized in her eyes, which will ensure that you grow as a person and that you become a better man in her eyes.

Advertisement for volunteer work on your Facebook? Better click apply now. Women have shown a fascination with men who do volunteer work. A study. 'Selflessness is sexy' reported helping behavior increases the desirability of men and women as long-term sexual partners. It showed that qualities of altruism in men made them more desirable as long-term partners (and vice versa.) The attractiveness in men also increased for short-term flings but not as considerably as for long-term relationships. The authors concluded that altruism maybe is linked to 'good genes' or parental care, which both sexes look for.

Task

To get the hang of the whole idea of being into hobbies, make a list of the three things that interest you the most. They could be anything from reading to exercising. List them down in order of 1,2, and 3. Then prioritize them by making number 1 the one that interests you the most.

This way, this short task will help you find out things that you are interested in. Keeping up the more metaphysical attractive traits related to passion is considered the least important. In a world motivated by hearing no evil see no evil maxim, **be a man who stands up for what he believes in**. It could be gay rights. It could be his favorite football team. It could even be something as mundane and equally as adorable as his dogs. Something that gives you passion and makes you become a better person is something that you would undoubtedly stand up for.

Seeing someone not scared of whatever other people might say about his opinions is incredibly sexy for a woman. A man who knows how to make a point is worth investing her time in.

Remember to be solid in your stance. She will be attracted to you.

Physical Appearance

Coming to the most controversial reason, this can be hard on some, and this especially requires you to read and understand the previous chapter about preparation. You are not offering much in the look department (of course I had to put subtly), this reason which requires more effort than the rest of the reasons. However, you might be lucky because women tend to look at physical appearances as lesser than men; this was also demonstrated by Men's health's survey wherein the "Top five physical traits of men "Sense of style (30%) was appreciated more than a handsome face (26%) or height (15%) or a muscular build (13%) or even fitness (12%)."

However, looking good is essential. Work on yourself; invest in yourself, which is why this book started with the advice of preparing yourself. Suppose you are overweight, control your diet, and hit the gym (Remember that your diet is more important than exercise). And **then be proud of your effort.** Remember that if there are things you truly cannot change about yourself, then there is no need to be insecure because the person you are looking for should accept your features beyond your control.

Insecurity is never sexy if circumstances are beyond your capabilities. You are not allowed to pity yourself. Although also realize that being over-confident about yourself is not that great either.

You need to maintain balance.

Personality

All this now brings us to the most important reason some people cannot find partners: personality. This reason is perhaps the hardest to accept; it is not easy to admit that you cannot find someone because your character is not that attractive because the issue is not with all those women or the situation but because it is you. If you feel slightly guilty right now, please accept it so you can move forward.

This reason definitely and usually tops the list. Women emphasize personality, and some common qualities are generally not desirable at all to them. Of course, some of such qualities should be understandable, without any need to mention them, such as physically abusing someone or being offensive and malicious. Let us discuss those bad qualities that men tend to overlook.

In 2015, YourTango, Chemistry.com, and MSN's Glo. com polled more than 20,000 people in the power of attraction and found out what women hated about men. These qualities included: Lack of personal hygiene, narcissism, immaturity, and lack of intelligence. According to Ranker's online survey (which had fifteen thousand votes), the worst qualities in men include dishonesty, cheating personality, being self-centered, inconsiderate, selfish, rude,and unreliable. Female Firsts' survey of "Most annoying male habits" includes:

- Not admitting when you are wrong.
- Never surprising the woman.
- Ignoring and staring at other women.

Of course, many disliked qualities might vary in women like some women hate smokers, and some women do not like men who wear skinny jeans. Some women might dislike men who complain ALL THE TIME. Whatever it is, generally bad personality is often the top reason why men cannot find women. Hence, before going any further, I recommend you perform your SWOT analysis (right now, yes do it).

Task

The SWOT analysis will not only help you in the field of relationships but in each field of life. Right now, you should perform a SWOT Analysis, which is particular to relationships.

1. List out your strengths, for example, kindness, being organized, or great height.

2. List out your weaknesses like arrogance or being overweight.

3. List out your opportunities. For instance, if you have joined a yoga club where you can find women or have free access to your college gym, those can be counted as your opportunities, as you have chances of socializing with women there.

4. List out threats, for example, other men (this is another reason you should avoid finding someone at the bar because a lot of other men are looking for the same there, increasing your threat and thus decreasing the probability of success.)

After knowing these, try to improve your strengths and increase your opportunities while at the same time working on your weaknesses to convert them into strengths. Avoid threats or challenge threats to be made into opportunities. An example of this can be that you improve your communication skills and sense of style so much that they make you stand out amongst other men. Thus, the other men will no longer be a threat. After evaluating yourself and knowing some of the mistakes you have been previously making, pause here again.

Remember to **Accept** your mistakes so that you can work on them.

Increase your odds with her

1. Seem busy doing important activities. If you have different things happening in your life, she will be intrigued to know you more.

2. Don't seem you want sex from her. Don't ruin your chances. If you want only sex, there are other ways.

3. Ask her questions that will excite her mind. Is there something you have dreamed of doing all your life? What's stopping you? she will open up to you if you ask this.

4. Get into her mind by asking, "If a crystal could tell you the truth about yourself and your life and future, what would you ask?"

5. Connect with her by asking, "If you could change anything about the way you were raised, what would it be?"

6. Make three 'we' statements. This is going to improve your chemistry. "We are both in this room feeling the power of love."

7. Poke her with this question – "if you were to die this evening, what would you regret most not having told someone? Why haven't you done it yet?"

8. Disagree with her. Show the courage to contradict her and come out as a confident man. It will earn you valuable points.

9. Challenge her. Don't be too available to her. Remain busy with your goals. Don't always run after her. Let her chase you.

10. Show you care. Get her small gifts. Call her up if she gets late from the office. Surprise her with your cooking skill.

Chapter 4

How To Fight Negative Feelings

"Life is 10% what happens to you and 90% how you react to it."
– Charles R. Swindoll

I remember someone looking at a "forever alone" meme on Facebook and initially laughing and then crying. Not finding someone for you can have several effects on you, especially if you want to have a partner. Some people may laugh at this phenomenon by saying, there are single men and women around the world, and most of them do not seem suicidal, so you are just over dramatic when you tell them that you are depressed because you cannot find someone. (Of course, men have a hard time confessing this too.) Be aware of the fact that this phenomenon of rejection can become serious.

Rejection is the 10%, and 90% is what you going to do afterward

This loneliness, according to Psychology Today, may just lead to chronic depression and even alcoholism, and in the worst case, even suicide. Psychologist John Cacioppo of the University of Chicago showed in his study that lonely people tend to be less helped by medical procedures as admitted by doctors and also tend to stress more. The key that I want to emphasize is that being in a relationship should not cure this loneliness. It can be cured by appreciating yourself and **surrounding yourself with people other than lovers, including friends and family**. I'll explain why I am mentioning this notion in a book made to advise relationships.

At times when I give relationship advice, I notice that at one point during the talk, men tend to seem even more depressed than they initially were. I do not know what it is. Maybe they realize that they are genuinely not good enough because they have most of the weaknesses I mentioned above.

This chapter is placed in this book only for that reason. I know, and I understand how difficult being single can be. Those late nights when your room is too silent, and you crave someone's presence, touch, or voice yet do not even have the power to admit this can be excruciating.

Those days when you finally accept to hang out with your friends, all of whom have partners, and come home regretting your decision can be as hard. The rainy days when you drive in your car alone, with weather perfect for excitement, wishing someone sat in the passenger seat you could reach out to can be tough too. I know people who lose themselves in solitude which is why you hear about someone committing suicide after a breakup, and at that moment, it sounds stupid when someone else does it, "I mean really, he killed himself because of a girl?" but know that loneliness, as it gets worst, may make you do things that might seem incredulous to others.

And this is what this book wants to cure by finding you, someone. However, remember that it is also as imperative to decrease these feelings of emptiness. **It should always be your priority number one to be happy with yourself**. These feelings of loneliness might make you feel completely alone, separate from the world. Know that these feelings arise because you forget you are always with the most important person you can be, and that is YOU. Yes, you. No matter how vague and non-concrete this answer sounds, this is the answer to your problems. You have not fallen in love with yourself. Learn to enjoy your company. Do things for yourself.

For example, dress up and treat yourself at a fancy restaurant, or go travel alone and enjoy it, read new books on those quiets nights and laugh out loud at yourself, tell yourself every day in the mirror that you love yourself, but you will love you even more if you improve and motivate yourself with that.

Unlearn to hate yourself.

And if at any moment sadness strikes, remember for the love of *all* that is great that you are not alone in this world and then have a fresh start. You might think that when I say love yourself, I will probably decrease your chances of finding and being happy in a relationship, but that is not true. As obvious as this sounds, people who love themselves tend to be happier, and people who tend to be happier manage to attract more people, and in the words of the famous blogger Ilana Donna Arazie,

> **"No one is ever going to love you more than you love yourself."**

In other words, until you're 100 percent into YOU, no one else will be…. I mean, think about it. If you're not connected to who you are, how the heck are you going to connect with someone else?

I remember one story of a girl who didn't seem to find a guy fit for her emotional needs. Every time she entered a relationship, she found herself happy during the first few months of their dating stage, and then things would change. She found herself ending up alone with lots of complaints and insecurity. Her friends tried to find the root cause of the problems and unhappiness.

This girl was not happy inside due to insecurity and lack of motivation to keep herself upbeat and alive even when she was not with someone. Learning that she came from a broken family and lacked emotional support as she grew up, she covered herself and the pain of going through one romantic relationship after another without much luck.

One cannot be entirely happy with someone without being happy with themselves first. I keep reiterating this point in the book because it is so important to get this. You cannot give what you don't have as simple as it is.

Find yourself first before you go out and find someone.

Task
Right now, stop everything you are doing and list 5 things you love about yourself. Do it right now! This is guaranteed to make you smile.

Now that you are getting to know yourself better, you will love to explore more.

Now keeping all of these lessons in mind, apply that confidence and self-love when you approach a girl. In the same way that you feel lonely and depressed, it is possible that the girl you approach may feel the same way. Make sure that when you approach someone, you do not become overconfident in your abilities or good looks. Speak to her like she is an equal and a respectable human being.

Do not use awkward and borderline rude pickup lines that your 'bros' tell you to work like a charm. They are disrespectful and are mostly used to objectify and belittle women. The more you respect a woman, the better she will treat you. With the kind of society that we live in, women are used to being catcalled and given all sorts of odd 'compliments' on a day-to-day basis. The difference between these compliments and the ones that are worth giving isthe way they are given. If you want to tell a woman, she looks lovely, say it in a way that makes her feel like you are not just saying it to get into her pants.

The bottom line: The way you talk to a lady can change a lot of things. This all comes from and is inexplicably linked to your self-worth. The tasks in this chapter will help you learn to appreciate yourself and also keep you grounded enough to ensure that when you speak to a woman, it is not in a derogatory manner.

Chapter 5

Break Down Her Trust Issues

" Trusting is hard. Knowing who to trust, even harder"
– Maria V. Snyder

A healthy relationship stands tall on trust and only trust. Once it's lost, it takes a while to rebuild it. But, it is not impossible. Breaking down your partner's trust issues requires consistent effort, genuine concern, and honesty.

When your partner has trust issues due to your past actions or her past experiences, the only thing you can do in this situation is to reassure her. But, reassure her about what exactly? As her man, you need to reassure her about your feelings for her, your intentions with her, whether she can trust you or not, and your attraction toward her.

So, what do you do to gain her trust?

Here is a list of things you can do to gain her trust and put an end to her trust issues.

1. Keep your word. (Say what you mean)
    Infidelity is not the only cause behind trust issues. You should not feel entitled to her trust just because you have not cheated on her. Maybe she does not trust you because you are unable to keep your word or fulfill promises. Now, think hard and try to remember every time you promised her something and did not keep your word. Maybe you forgot to get her the dress you promised her or avoided something you said you would do for her, or maybe it slipped your mind. Sure, you were not spiteful, but the reality is that your girl has trust issues when it comes to you.

    So, if that is the case, then you need to make an effort to be mindful of the effort to make promises you can keep.

2. Give her the password to your phone.
    Allowing your partner access to your phone seems weird at first. But, building and gaining your significant other's trust, especially after your actions have bruised it, requires effort. Besides, if you have nothing on your phone that you have to hide, what's the issue? If giving your girl access to your phone helps her trust you more, then so be it.

It is understandable if you want to create healthy boundaries in your relationship and think that giving access to something as personal as your phone invades that boundary. But, it depends on how you handle the situation. Trust issues can be dealt with in a healthy way. If you seem hesitant, she will always think you have something to hide and might even check your phone behind your back. This is the point where your relationship starts to get unhealthy. So, be chill when you give your girl the password to your phone. Treat it like it is no big deal, and she will never consider it necessary to go through your phone behind your back and invade your privacy. -

3. Be consistent.

   Being inconsistent and flakey, especially when it comes to something as fragile as trust, can do more damage than you think. You don't want her to assume that you are not genuine with your efforts and that maybe you were trying to get something out of them.

   So, no matter how hard the day gets, take a breather and remain consistent. Otherwise, all your efforts shall go to waste, and you will have to start from scratch.

4. Be your true self in front of her.

   If you want to break down her trust issues, you not only have to be your true self in front of her but also with others. Chances are if she already has trust issues with you and she finds you acting bizarrely different in front of others, she will have a more challenging time trusting you even when you are being genuine when alone with her. Besides, being your true self is the easiest person to be. You don't have to keep up with an "image," nor do you have to play a character.

5. Don't be afraid to express your true intentions.
   Honesty and authenticity are shown through expressing your true intentions. Be honest about your intentions with them, about the ideal pace of the relationship (especially if it is new), your priorities, and everything you consider important for the relationship.

6. Don't rush things.
   You can't rush it when building trust. If you do, your partner would assume that you consider yourself entitled to her trust. So, be patient and don't let your restlessness ruin a good relationship for the both of you.

7. Tell her something personal that you have never told anyone.
   When you become vulnerable before your girl, you are able to connect with each other on another level. Moreover, she will feel important in your life and

someone whom you trust wholeheartedly. The more welcomed she feels in your life, the more she will trust you.

8. Lead her to the right decisions.
Whenever she comes to you for advice, always guide her in a way that benefits her. If she feels that your advice is more catered to you than her, she will most likely hide things from you, bottle up her feelings, and grow distant. So, the next time she asks you if she should get a job that pays her more than yours, be genuinely happy for her and give her the right advice. Show that you are focused on her growth, whether the relationship lasts or not. She will trust you more than ever when she can see your genuine care and concern for her.

9. Don't be scared to let her in on your flaws.
Why? Well, because she will trust you more. Typically, people tend to hide their flaws so that the other person does not use them against them. But, that is no way to live. The more comfortable you feel sharing your flaws with your girl, the more comfortable she will do the same.

The bottom line is that it is very much possible to repair a relationship and rebuild trust. Now, whether it's worthwhile depends on the demands of your relationship. A healthy relationship is always worth saving. It is completely understandable if your partner has trust issues and requires a lot of reassurance. Being there for her when the relationship is not rainbows and flowers shows your commitment to her. Your willingness to reassure her will also considerably help break down her trust issues. If you decide to try mending things, be aware that it will take some time. If both parties are devoted to the process of restoring trust, you may discover that you both emerge stronger than before, together as a couple and as individuals as well.

"Trust is the glue of life. It's the most essential ingredient in effective communication. It's the foundational principle that holds all relationships."
– Stephen R. Covey

10 things girls hate about guys
1. Being too nice. She doesn't want you to be too nice or perfect. A little naughty will be great.

2. Being insecure and doubting yourself. Girls don't want to be with someone who is not sure of themselves. If you suspect your own ability, how can you keep her happy?

3. Text them long paragraphs and double text. How can you spend hours writing long paras and double texting someone? It is so annoying.

4. Too clingy men. This is an absolute no-no. No woman likes a man who clings to her.

5. Too emotional men. Handling emotions is a marker of maturity, and women don't like men who are full of feelings.

6. Always chilling. Spending your life only chilling and not having enough activities puts off women.

7. Treat women with respect. Women don't want any special treatment from men. Be friends with them, like you treat your male friends.

8. Not being funny. Who wants to spend time with a grumpy face? Guys who are not funny don't score well with gals.

9. Treat women like a celebrity. Making them sit on a pedestal will make her uncomfortable.

10. Lying to them. It is unacceptable. It is misleading and shows your lack of integrity.

Chapter 6

Yin and Yang

If you aren't ready for rejection, you aren't ready for love.
– Marty Rubin

I want to share a story from my dating experience here. It happened a few years ago. I knew a lot of girls and Natany was one of them for whom I developed feelings. So, I invited her to my house, and I was super excited when she agreed to come over. It was a Friday night. I cleaned my apartment and even vacuum cleaned the bathroom as I know girls are impressed by these.

At around 8 o'clock,Natany called me to inform me that she had arrived but could not locate my home. So, I went out to fetch her. Natany's friend Alexa was waiting with her, and she assured us she would pick her up after some time.

We came to my apartment and spent the next couple of hours chatting. I liked her company but didn't feel any sexual urge.

I noticed that after that visit, her texts became fewer and fewer. I couldn't understand what was wrong. I was an **absolute gentleman** with her, then why she was avoiding me? Then it hit like a stone!

I realized I was too nice to her and that frustrated her. I wanted to be an exception and didn't try to make out with her. That backfired as Natany expected something else from me.

So, boys, **don't try to be too nice to girls**; show your bad side as well. If any girl takes interest in you, don't just sit and chat. Pull her legs, make fun of her, or crack jokes on others and show her that you are an interesting person to spend time with. However, don't go overboard with your jokes, as she may not appreciate them. When you like a girl, show her your feelings, but be normal with her. Don't put her on a pedestal; girls actually don't look for such treatment.

I told you about Natany to highlight an interesting but less discussed aspect of dating- showing both your good and bad sides. You must have read hundreds of love stories in which the guy is shown either as good or bad. Dating blogs and popular beliefs teach us that girls love bad guys. Hence, in most films, girls fall for bad guys. On the other hand, there is another perspective that good guys always win.

However, in real life, no one is purely good or bad. We are neither black nor white but different shades of grey, which makes us appealing and unique. Here lies the importance of the concept of yin and yang. Are you wondering what yin and yang have to do with dating? Let me explain.

The ancient Chinese concept of yin and yang
Yin and yang stand for duality. They represent two opposite characters residing in harmony. Yin and yang are represented in a diagram as a disc with two parts – white and black. It is known as taijitu in China. The symbol has a circle composed of two interlocking teardrops or swirls, each having a dot of opposite color inside. Yin is the dark side that represents negativity and coldness. It is the feminine force. On the other hand, yang is the white part that stands for positivity, softness, and masculinity.

If you observe the circle, you will find two connected waves with the crest as yang and the trough as yin.

The profound meaning of the symbol has a strong influence on every aspect of our lives. The opposite characters represented by yin and yang complement each other. They exist in dichotomy and signify the interconnectedness of the world. As we often say, light cannot exist without dark, similarly, yin cannot live without yang. Like waves, yin and yang flow into each other, influencing and modifying each other. Together they symbolize interdependence, the negativity cannot exist without positivity, light cannot survive without shadow, and warmth cannot live without coldness.

Importance of yin and yang in our lives

The symbol of yin yang shows that there is no marked division between the two forces. Together they look whole; if yin expands, yang has to contract and vice versa. We achieve harmony when they are equal and reach the ideal situation.

This brings us to a vital question – what is the significance of yin and yang in our lives? Why am I speaking about them in this book?

We are all like the taijitu symbol; a little evil exists in us along with goodness. Sometimes, the bad overpowers the good, at other times, the good suppress the evil. None of us are purely good or bad. We are a little of both, making us unique.

Now coming to dating, Natany rejected me or was disappointed because I was only decent to her. If I expressed my clever side, she might have been intrigued.

What I learned from this experience is that along with behaving well with girls and showing them respect, we have to let them have a sneak peek into our evil side.

We can achieve this by cracking jokes, pulling their legs, and laughing at our follies.

The so-called bad guys can win over women by showing their good side. They can show their sensitivity or a warm heart to impress their women. Whatever image you project on women, always maintain a balance; that's what yin and yang teach us.

If we behave all virtuous, the women will get bored. On the other hand, if we are only nasty to them, they may misunderstand us. So, let your dark side out to pique their interest.

My friends, keep this in mind next time you meet a gal. Don't be too good or too bad. Present a balance of these, like yin and yang, and see how girls fall in love head over heels for you.

Chapter 7

Taking Action

"Setting goals is the first step in turning the invisible into the visible."
Tony Robbins

After analyzing yourself, you now know what you need to improve before you proceed forward. Now it can be confusing about how to approach improvement, what exactly should you do to improve, right?

Taking Action
Remember not to think you have improved if you have not done **something practical.** If your improvement is abstract and you are thinking right now, "Oh yes, I do ignore people at times, but now that I know this, I will just pay a little more attention next time."

When will that next time be, man?

This notion makes your improvement abstract because you haven't done anything, so you cannot cross that off the list. Make it a point to eliminate this from your life. Message people, you are usually in contact with, apologize to them for being a little ignorant, ask them about their lives and listen, listen to them with your full attention.

Remember, the first step is the toughest, but then it gets easier. The steps that you take to decrease your weaknesses will be your **progress**. And making a habit of that progress will eventually turn it into strength.

Let us consider another example. Perhaps you realize that you do not have a good sense of style. So, call up a friend who always manages to look fly and receives compliments or stares of approval or follow fashion models on social media. Take help from both outlets to improve your dress sense. Use social media for inspiration, and take help from your stylish friend to approve of your style, and maybe give you some more tips. You can also take inspiration from Pinterest, fashion blogs, and fashion YouTube channels to learn how to style different pieces of clothing together and carry them effortlessly.For instance, if you recognize that your major flaw is your arrogance, look for ways to humble yourself. Try to remain mindful and catch yourself whenever you are about to act arrogantly or make a statement that comes from an arrogant mindset. According to the Huffington Post, genuine, meaningful compliments, giving credit to others, admitting mistakes, and attempting to learn about people; their names and some of their distinguishing characteristics not only counter an arrogant mindset but also make you appear friendly, humble, and more welcoming.

I will share some advice on how to become attractive through the means of communication. Listen well. In practical dating advice, you must pay attention to the other person while you are on a date by keeping eye contact and being keen on details that the other person is giddy about telling you about. It is a big plus point if you know how to pay attention and listen well. Some guys with great egos somewhat find it challenging to speak less and listen more as they think they have so much to say to attract a woman, but the truth is, women are more attracted to you when actions are seen rather than what they vaguely hear from you. They'd rather listen to their girly chit-chat once in a while than hear you bragging about something.

Similarly, when it comes to your weaknesses, choose to focus on eradicating them one by one from your life. If your issues are internal and related to your circumstances, such as financial instability, then even though the process might be excruciatingly slow, it will still not lead to an ugly dead end. So, don't be afraid to start. Each day, take baby steps and put one foot in front of the other, and eventually, you will accomplish every mountain.Remember, long-lasting change doesn't come overnight (nothing great ever does). Your motivating factors, as mentioned in Chapter One, should be strong enough to keep you consistent throughout your journey and help you progress forward. Tracking your progress by consulting people and asking them to tell you if they have noticed any visible change in you can prove to be effective. Don't shy away from treating yourself a little and appreciating your efforts when you and those around you notice progress.

One thing I can tell you for sure is that if this self-development still does not help you, for some very peculiar reason, to find a partner even then, it will make you a better soul. There will be nothing to lose. But if the situation is a normal one, relax, good people, attract good people.

Task

So here is one challenge for you. Write three letters to yourself. The first is the two things you will eliminate from your life in three months. When you do, congratulate yourself if you have eliminated those things. If not, write the second letter to yourself committing to change, and if both things were removed from the first letter, set yourself two new challenges and check back in three months. Once you get the hang of it, you will no longer need a letter to remind you to eliminate habits that may be a hindrance to finding a meaningful relationship.

Use Her Name Often

A good tip for talking to a woman is for you to use her name. Now, this may sound pretty weird at first because randomly saying someone's name is incredibly awkward. There is, however, a cool way to use this technique. When referring to her or telling her anything, use her name clearly and distinctly. What exactly does this accomplish? It builds a **connection**; it makes her special; it changes the whole dimension when added to a sentence.

For example:
"Kate, your views are interesting."
"Kate, I hope you like the cupcake."

Or say her name, like it has a secret attached to it, "Kate..." or "Kate you..." and she'll badger you about what it was that you were going to say, but look at her without responding. This shows her that you are paying attention to her, giving value to her, focusing on her directly and that you are attracted to her. It can sound very sexy when someone else takes your name while looking you in the eye and conversing with you. Dr. Lindsay Henderson, PsyD, reveals that using someone's name makes them feel validated, important, and closer to you. Furthermore, everything you convey using their name will find a firmer place in their minds. They will always remember how you made them feel. So, always use her name when you want her to be more open, honest, and attentive towards you, and make sure you use her name, especially when youare complimenting her.

3 GUARANTEED WAYS TO MAKE HER FALL FOR YOU FAST

1. Become her cheerleader.

   Nothing makes a woman fall harder for a man who supports her religiously. The trick is to not only support her when she needs it, but also hype her up when she is trying to accomplish something. So, for instance, if you go out for adventure sports, hype her up when she is climbing a wall, or driving an ATV, etc. Now, you don't have to take her on an extreme adventure, so you can win her heart by becoming her "hype man." All you need to do is be there for her, encourage her, show her the brighter side when she is wallowing in self-doubt, and support her in her daily life without becoming a pushover. When she is doing something wrong, call her out on it with a firm yet kind stance. When you succeed in this, you will notice that she constantly not only looks at you for validation and support but looks up to you with respect.

2. Give her special treatment.

   Through your actions, show her that she is special to you. This can be done by giving her special attention.

However, you don't necessarily have to take her out on extravagant dates every week or shower her with huge bouquets. Use simple actions instead, and build on them with time. For starters, without making it too obvious (because a little mystery is necessary), tell her how bad you are at texting people back because of your busy schedule, but always respond to her within a reasonable time, such as within an hour. This simple act will make her feel incredibly special in your life. You can also show her she is special by sharing her favorite songs, books, or movies with her. Over time, you can treat her to more special things so that she appreciates them. If you are too nice too soon, she will soon lose respect and value in her eyes.

3. Let her miss you.

   How will her heart yearn for you if you are ALWAYS around her? Get yourself busy with your career, don't neglect your friends and family, and while you are busy with your stuff, let her miss you. Stepping away from time to time does not mean you outright ignore her. **Just be busy**, and if you are together, then inform her if you are going to be busy that day.

SIDE NOTE

If she texts you what you are doing or anything between the line, reply with something exciting if you are not a white-collar won't hurt.

Connect

Last but not least, if you invite a girl out to chill with you, be very calm and collected when you do so. If she says she has plans already, respect that instead of insisting. This will show her that you are a gentleman who respects women. If you invite her once and she has plans, then try again after some time. If she has 'plans' yet again or declines, then DON'T CALL HER AGAIN. This will show her that you are respectable and don't go around chasing girls everywhere. If anything, this will make her respect you more.

Let her be. But, always be polite. You don't want to seem ingenuous as all you wanted was to hang out with her, and now that she has declined, you vanish from her life. Be around, but stop asking her to hang out. Post cool stories of you having fun with your friends and living your best life. In the meantime, make her feel more comfortable around you. Eventually, she will reach out to you. However, if she doesn't, you should make a move again. Invite her to something she will enjoy wholeheartedly. Now that you know her better, finding an activity will not be hard. When deciding on a date, ask about her schedule and give her an overview of yours. Remember, don't mention a date because if you do, she has an easy way to deny you. Go on a date she gives you since she will not be "busy."

Apply all these techniques, but always remember that women are not play things.Make an effort to **show her respect** in everything you do and say to her.Work on becoming a hardworking and respectable man, and women will love you for this.

Dating tips

1. Come prepared with good questions
2. Scope out the restaurant menu before you to there (pick a restaurant in your budget)
3. Don't sit across from her. It'll be a little awkward when both of you don't have anything to say.
4. **Let her do most of the talking**. This will allow you to understand her and know more about her likes and dislikes.
5. Choose an apt environment (Introvert tend to thrive when in low ley environments, I know cause I'm one of them)
6. **Stay true to yourself**. Don't act to be someone else as eventually as it will hurt in the future.
7. Compliment her for small things. She will be happy to know that you take keen notice. (Don't over do it)
8. Absolutely have a way out of the date if need be.
9. Do something new on every date. Try a new café, a new genre of music, or visit a museum or library in your locality.
10. Smell well when you meet her. Personal hygiene is **very important**, so take care of yourself.
11. Never be late on a date. If you cannot reach her on time, text her, and apologize when you meet.

Chapter 8

Pre Sex Tips

---

*"The deepest moments of intimacy occur
when you're not talking."*
- Patricia Love

Do you want to get the most pleasure out of the night while making sure she also gets her fill?

People think that being better at sex happens when you're physically strong, but in my experience and the research I did, I found that it is more of a mental game than a physical game.

Having good and lasting sex is a skill, and like any skill, it can be learned and perfected.

Let me show you how you can step up your sex game and take your relationship to new heights.

Here are some ways to last longer in bed and have her craving for more.

Engage in foreplay

If sex means having a good dream, then ejaculation means waking up. The more you try to stay in the dream zone, the more you will enjoy the experience.

Try out something more than just regular penetration.

You can be creative and explore the different kinks you and your partner have.

Foreplay not only delays ejaculation but makes your sexual experience much more exciting. Foreplay can mean different things to different people, so you can explore your own desires and your partner's fantasies to see what gives you the best high. Try blindfolds, anal, and oral sex, and the possibilities are endless.

Here are some ways you can engage in foreplay and warm up before the main event. You can try to:

- Invite your partner to dance.
- Give your partner a sensual massage.
- Watch a sexy movie together.
- Explore kinks and new sex toys with your partner.
- Take a bath together.
- Sexting throughout the day.
- Take your time removing the articles of clothing.
- Pretend to be someone else, like a pizza delivery guy, plumber, some guy down the road, etc.
- Engage in BDSM.

And the possibilities are endless. It all depends on what you and your partner want. Have it figured out, and it will make your night truly remarkable.

Learn the pause-squeeze method.
Let's use the example of marathons to clarify how it works. If you keep on running without giving your body a rest, it is more likely that your muscles will give out, and you'll find yourself finished way before your mark.

Instead, experienced marathoners do that every eight to nine minutes; they stop running and take one to two-minute walk breaks where they slow down.

When you have regained enough of their stamina, you'll get back in the game and continue running. You'll keep on repeating this pattern till you reach their goal.

The pause-squeeze method works the exact same way. It can be done while masturbating or having sex.

You can use it during masturbation to get the hang of it, and once you're familiar with the technique, you can start using it during sex.

Here's how it works.
1. Continue having sex in a normal way until you feel that you're about to ejaculate.

2. When you feel like you can't hold it in any longer, pull out and start squeezing the tip of your penis with your thumb until the need to ejaculate passes.
3. By pushing the tip of your penis, you stop the flow and let it rest.
4. When that feeling to ejaculate fades away, you get back into it, continue having sex and repeat the technique as needed.

Practice staying calm during sex.
Sex anxiety is something real that many people can experience during intercourse. Not being able to relax during sex can keep you from enjoying the full experience and may even affect the quality of your erection.

Fortunately, some ways can help you keep your cool and not let your anxieties get the best of you during sex.

1. If your mind is going all over the place, the simplest way to get the hang of yourself is to **breathe**. Shifting your focus on your breathing can detach you from the insecurities and anxieties going inside your head and bring you back to the here and now. **One tip I use that effective to last longer in bed is to inhale from your mouth and exhale from your mouth. It'll help you concentrate on your breathing**.

2. During sex, you drop all the layers between you and your partner. If something bothers you, there is no better way to have it sorted out than communicating with your partner. If a drifting mind is your thing, just tell it to your partner so they become aware of it and don't take it as a negative gesture.

3. Engage your full senses and see how each part of your body feels. During sex, start scanning your body from head to toe and experience how the muscles in your body feel. Feel your partner's touch, the relaxation or tension in your muscles. The more mindful you become, the more you'll stay engaged in sex and not have your mind wander elsewhere.

Use mental distraction
It's an old classic but highly effective. During sex, try to focus on something non-erotic. You can think of it as the mental equivalent of the pause-squeeze method.

The way I use it is that when I'm about to ejaculate, I imagine driving my car in reverse.

This reduces the enjoyment of the act itself, but it delays my ejaculation.

When I assign my brain to some other thought, my sexual flow decreases. And when it's low enough, I start focusing back on sex and get another chance to enjoy the experience all over again.

Exercise can work wonders.
After my ex-girlfriend and I broke up, I was working out constantly. I became more focused on myself.

I worked out after getting off working my night shift. My workout wasn't for that long. I probably worked for 30 minutes, which would eventually lead to burnout.

Here's what I did:
Fortunately, there are specific exercises that can help you strengthen your pelvic region.

1. Pull-ups (all grips pull-ups) if you can't do anymore, hold the position until you fall.
2. Push-ups (wide and diamonds) if you can't do anymore, hold the position until you fall.
3. One set of planks (hold the position until you fall)

The stronger your pelvic muscles are, the more you can delay your ejaculation.

Two weeks after my breakup, my ex came to my place to " talk."

We got to talking, then touching, then kissing. You can imagine what happened next.

I used to be a minute-man before I started the 30mins workout, but after I laid it down, I felt strong and lasted longer than I expected. That's when I noticed a turning point in my sex game.

Chapter 9

Outer voices – don't let people's opinions damage your relationship

"If you fuel your journey on the opinions of others, you are going to run out of gas."
~ Steve Maraboli

When John moved in with Larissa, his friends didn't support him. Some of them went ahead to warn John as they thought Larissa was not the right match for him. Thankfully, John didn't listen to the naysayers and started staying with his girlfriend. He dared to ignore the outer voices that kept on criticizing his decision. However, it is not easy to stand against the reproach we face from our near ones. External opinions matter a lot in our lives and often ruin our happiness. How do you recognize the negative outer voices and stay alert against them? How do you stop them from ruining your relationship?

The interfering people – how their points of view damage our relationships

You love to spend special days like birthdays and anniversaries at home, but since all your friends go out and share photos on social media, you also do that unwillingly. I have seen many people fall for this peer pressure. This gets worse when your friends start commenting on your personal choices like eating habits or sense of fashion.

I knew a couple who adopted minimalistic living and chose not to splurge on dresses and fancy items. Their friends commented openly on their lifestyle, and that strained their relationship. Again, you will find relatives showing interest in your personal lives and showing their disapproval. Maybe, they are concerned about your future, but they never realize that by expressing their points of view, they are causing you stress.

So, we need to recognize these negative outer voices that slowly poison our minds and damage our relationships.

Asking too many questions is another way in which the outer voices influence our relationships. When we were single, we received undue attention from our relatives and friends. After getting into a relationship, these people start asking us when we will settle down. Achieving relationship milestones is a personal issue, but these people make it a race and expect us to follow a pattern.

We usually hang out with like-minded people, and when they express their doubts about our relationships, we cannot take that lightly. Since friends play a powerful role in our lives, their views and concerns matter to us. It is hard to ignore the worries they raise, and this strains our relationship.

Some people may force you to get into relationship competition and create unnecessary stress in your life. When your bestie celebrates her 5th anniversary in an exotic place and asks you about your anniversary plans, you feel like copying her. The external forces compel us to overlook the beauty of our bonding and start showing off. Recognizing them on time and staying away from such opinions will help your relationship bloom.

Seeking the approval of others is our general psychology, but when it comes to relationships, this may do you more harm than good. The people around you may disapprove of your relationship as it doesn't fit their background. This problem becomes more pronounced when you are in an intercultural relationship. Please stop comparing your experience with others and seeking their consent. Celebrate your uniqueness and the bond you have created with your partner.

This brings us to a vital question; how do we stop the outer voices from interfering in our lives?

How to handle the outer voices?

Before moving ahead, I want to make a point here. Cutting off toxic people from our lives is a good thing. However, it is not always possible to keep these people at bay. Our relatives, colleagues, and friends may all be in this category. It is also true that people close to us make negative comments to express their concern for us. Friends who worry too much may also voice their opinions in a negative way. Talk to that friend or close relative and tell them how their negativity is affecting you personally. Try to dissipate their concern by sharing how happy you are with your partner.

In most cases, it is better to ignore external criticism. Let them make snide remarks, there is no need to react if you are not bothered by them.

There will be meddlesome people who don't understand the subtle gesture. If you find them voicing their discontent openly, and if you feel disturbed by this unpleasant behavior, it is time to take a stand. Retorting back with a befitting answer is enough to stop these waging tongues. It is essential to make these people realize the damage they are doing with their toxic remarks.

Share these issues with your partner. This will help you reduce your stress and find a better way to fight it off. Maybe, your partner is also facing a similar predicament, and together you can devise a way to stop these people.

If nothing works, you may have to cut off all ties with these toxic people. It is better to bid goodbye to those who constantly deride you with their toxic comments.

We all face ups and downs in a relationship and need to share our worries with others. However, vent out your feelings to very close friends who understand you. Share your views with only those who support you and always stand by you.

Outside influencers will not get a chance to demean you if you maintain a united front. Show your support for your partner, grow an unbreakable bond with your loved one, and this will deter anyone from opening their mouth against you.

Grow the courage to stand apart

We cannot expect others to understand or appreciate the choices we make in our lives. Intercultural or interracial relationships get attention from people as they do not fit the ideas people harbor in their minds. However, your conviction and courage should be strong to counter the questions people raise. It is not easy to stand apart from the crowd, but once you take a stance and stick to it, you will find people lauding you.

Whether you find people negating your feelings or commenting on your relationship, always remember that they have a right to express their views, and you have the right to ignore them.

Chapter 10

Too good to leave, too bad to stay – how to deal with bad relationships?

"Love is supposed to lift you up, not hold you down. It is supposed to push you forward, not hold you back."
~ **Suzy Kassem**

It took Olivia some time to find out that Evan was a compulsive liar. He lied about small things, like what he ate for lunch, how much he spent on drinks, or with whom he went for a match. Whenever Olivia confronted him, he got into fits of anger. Slowly, their relationship soured. Olivia felt sad but didn't leave Evan. She knew about his troubled childhood and thought that with love and patience, he would change one day. She was too much in love with Evan but was not happy with him either.

What is a bad relationship?
Do you think Olivia is stuck in a bad relationship? Should she leave Evan? It is not easy to identify a

toxic relationship. Most of us think a relationship is unhealthy if there is abuse, violence, or harassment. But things can be subtle too. If you are sad in a relationship, if it makes you anxious, stressed out, or angry, it is toxic for you. A relationship may start on the right note but stop bringing you joy after some time. If you experience persistent unhappiness, it is an evil union for you.

Whether you will continue in such a bond is up to you. No one can advise you on that. What we can do is help you identify the red flags in a relationship and let you know that it is harmful to you.

What are the signs of a bad relationship?
There are many, to begin with. As we said earlier, physical or verbal abuse and violence are broad markers of toxicity.

Relationships in which we experience volatility are usually bad for us. In this kind of relationship, you will find highs followed by lows that leave you stressed, anxious, and pensive. You don't know what to expect and how to avoid pain. Uncertainty is bad for us; it increases stress. So, relationships with doubts at such acute levels are not good. They are harmful to our well-being.

Is this a 'joke'?
Do you feel bad when your partner cracks a joke about how bad you are in reading directions? Does your

partner always make negative comments about your cooking skill or habit of forgetting things? If a joke leaves you feeling belittled, angry, humiliated, and stupid, IT IS NOT A JOKE. It is emotional bullying. A relationship where such bullying happens persistently is definitely toxic.

Are you afraid of your partner?

A healthy relationship is built on trust. If you are hiding anything from your partner lest he gets angry, you are stuck in a bad union. Do you hide whom you are meeting for lunch? Do you think he will get jealous if you go for a movie? These are red flags of an unhealthy relationship.

Why do people stay in bad relationships?

If you look around, you will find many people continuing in unhappy bonds. Why do they stay in a toxic relationship? The reasons vary from fear and unworthiness to lack of confidence.

Firstly, many people have low self-worth. Since they don't love themselves, they cannot honor their feelings also. They deny the right to respect and love and remain in unhealthy relationships as they are unsure of what they deserve.

This mostly happens with people who had a troubled childhood and were treated poorly by their parents or relatives.

Fear is a strong feeling. People dread being alone, judged, or ridiculed. The fear of an uncertain future also makes some remain in a bad relationship.

People who have been too long in an unhappy relationship get accustomed to it. This may sound strange, but the truth is they find the abuse normal. So, they live in pain but do not dare to quit. Despite being miserable, they continue in the relationship.

People continue in abusive relationships for the sake of children. They want to protect their children from the pain and torture of a divorce. They also fear that the children may accuse them of breaking the family.

Suffering from anguish, humiliation, and dejection for a prolonged time makes people lose all hope. The toxicity poisons their heart and mind to such an extent that there is no room left for dreams and love. Thus, they surrender to the situation and continue to suffer.

Financial comfort may make some people stay back with an abusive partner. They get used to the lifestyle and security and hence, decide to remain in the unhappy liaison.

I have seen couples where mutual dependence forces them to stick together. The suffering partner doesn't want to leave the abusive partner as he or she may feel alone. In certain cases, mental illnesses like depression or bipolar disorder may force a partner to stay back and take care of the partner. Some people may not have the nerve to let anyone suffer in rejection.

Should you continue with the relationship or quit?
At the end of the day, the call is yours. Whether you would remain trapped in an unhappy situation or have the nerve to strike back and leave is a personal choice.

If it is an old relationship with high emotional baggage, you may not be able to decide quickly. You can resort to counseling and medical care to help your partner rectify his behavior. Maybe your friends or relatives can help you appreciate the situation and make you believe in love again. If you have kids, you have to discuss them before making any decision.

For new relationships, it is easier to leave as the stakes are not high.

Never lose hope; that's the only message we want to give you. Thinking that everything is lost and you don't deserve to feel better will engulf you in plight. Seek help from friends and relatives to find a way out. You can stay back with renewed hope or love or leave to protect your self-esteem. Whatever you decide, be happy. Always remember that your happiness matters the most.

Chapter 11

How to identify red flags in women

"If you ignore the red flags, embrace the heartache to come."
–Amanda Mosher

'Why do you call so many times when I am with my friends? Don't you realize it's irritating!" Rex thought she was concerned and called to check where he was. Initially, he tried to explain to Maria that it looked odd when she called him up every two minutes to know where he was. However, no amount of explaining and reasoning could change her behavior. She continued to check out whenever he went with his friends to watch soccer or for dinner. Slowly, Max started losing his temper, and one day they broke up.

Does this sound familiar to you? Do you think Max should have identified the red flag before and saved himself from heartbreak?

Now, before we suggest what Max should have done or judge what is wrong with Maria, let us understand what a red flag is. Why is it important to identify it in the beginning?

What is a red flag? Why should you take them seriously?
A red flag is an indicator that tells us something is not right. It is intuitive and hence, not easy to decipher. In most cases, what seems okay from the outside is an issue of major concern for the parties involved. Maria's overprotective behavior toward Max may seem romantic in the initial stage of dating, but it is hard to put up with it when you are in a relationship for a long period.

It is difficult to identify red flags as the relationship may be going well, and we tend to ignore small issues that crop up occasionally. Actually, what gives us clues is our feelings, or to be more specific, our gut feelings. Your husband forgetting your birthday once may upset you, however, if you notice him ignoring important dates repeatedly, there is a cause for concern.

Apart from noticing such repeated behavior, check how you are feeling. If you feel uncomfortable, there is a reason to worry. Moreover, to get sure of a red flag, contemplate deeper to find out whether you are feeling uncared for, unsafe, or bad about yourself. If you answer any one of these positively, you are in a red flag zone.

Red flags are hard to identify when we start dating someone as the excitement around a new relationship is high, and we tend to overlook the small details. However, with time, these red flags start meddling with peace of mind; they may make you unhappy and eventually affect the relationship.

What are the most common red flags you must be aware of?

Have you started dating someone and are afraid of red flags? Do you wish to know what are the most common red flags in women? Here is a list of red flags we have commonly found in women.

She criticizes your acts

Everyone has their faults, and it is okay to complain about them. But if your partner criticizes you and makes you feel bad, you must take note of this. Using someone as a punching bag is not okay.

She always defends herself

We all make mistakes, and the best thing to do is say sorry and move on. However, some women get defensive and always blame others. This creates tension in a relationship. Conflicts become common as no one will take the blames, and hence you must look out for this red flag.

Mocking or disrespecting you

What is she mocks you for your slightest of mistakes? Does she disrespect you when you are discussing any problem? These are red flags. Pay attention to them and take necessary actions to save yourself from feeling bad later on.

She stonewalls you
Some women are efficient in doing this. Instead of conversing with you on any issue, she acts busy and evades talking. This shows she is incapable of rational discussions. It is up to you to decide how to handle such behavior.

She badmouths her ex
Now, there can be different forms of this problem. If you find your partner smacking her ex on the first date, you must take this seriously. When you are together for some time, and your mate badmouths all her exes, there is something to bother. If she does this to others, she will do this to you too.

She is texting you all the time
It is okay to message you about small things to show love, but what if it hampers your work routine? How will you handle your deadlines if your girlfriend messages you every hour and expects you to answer immediately?

Being a drama queen
Ever since she walked into your life, you feel like being a part of a soap opera. Some women are such drama queens that they can make your life hell. These women

believe everyone has a vendetta against them. This red flag is so irritating that you may want to run away from her.

Okay, so you know how to identify red flags now. What are you going to do if your babe has any of these? Well, there are two options. If it is a mild one, you can sit and discuss it with her. If both of you are serious about the relationship, you can solve the problem by discussing it. However, if she refuses to acknowledge her problem or blames you for her behavior, you may have to take a final call. The decision will be yours; what we want to stress is that at the end of the day, you should feel happy and valued. If a relationship makes you tense, unhappy, and unsafe, you must leave it.

Chapter 12

Would you be happy? How to have an exciting and loving relationship

---

"I wake up thinking of yesterday. The joy is in remembering; the pain is in knowing it was yesterday."
~ David Levithan

Kaine feels something is missing in his love life, but he cannot figure it out. When he started dating Chloe a year back, everything seemed perfect. She was besotted with Kaine and went out of her way to please him. Nowadays, when she goes out with him, she looks disinterested. She doesn't do any makeup nor make any effort to look good. Kaine feels she is bored or doesn't love him anymore. Is Chloe cheating Kaine?

There are plenty of couples like Kaine and Chloe. When they fell in love, everything seemed perfect. They showered each other with attention; they spent every waking hour together and never imagined living apart. However, a few years down the line, the relationship loses its sheen. They stop going on dates, they lose interest in talking, and even sex becomes a routine. Why do you think relationships get boring? Why do people stop caring for each other? Do people cheat because they miss the spark in their relationships?

Why does a relationship get boring?

Although every relationship is different, we still observe a pattern in them. When we get into a relationship, we have doubts and apprehensions. There are many risks like losing the person, not being good enough, or making mistakes. Are we wasting time? Is he the right one for me? These doubts preoccupy our minds. So, we are always on our guard and present our best selves.

The insecurity makes the game thrilling. The chase is so exciting; it creates an invigofeeling. That's love.

However, with time, the butterflies in our stomachs stop fluttering. As we come to know the person, the insecurities subside too. The relationship becomes stable, and we no longer fear losing the person. We get comfortable in each other's company and get casual. We achieve stability in the relationship.

However, the stability kills the fun. We don't chase our love interest anymore; rather we take her for granted. We have bills to pay, deadlines to achieve, and the stress of everyday life shifts our focus. As a result, we stop investing in the relationship. We don't go out for dates, we stop taking care of our looks, and even sex becomes a routine.

The problem arises when our partners start feeling neglected. Like Kaine, they feel depressed and unloved. As the spark dies in one relationship, we start looking for it elsewhere. Yes, you are right. Most people resort to cheating to spice up their love life.

How do we know your relationhip is getting boring?

Nothing happens overnight. Relationships get into a rut slowly, and if you are careful, you can identify the signs. So, what are the signs of a boring relationship?

Lack of interest – If you no longer want to know what's happening in your partner's life, there is a case for concern. We may lose interest in our partner's social life or office because we are too busy with our problems. People also lose interest when they have nothing in common to talk about.

Stop paying attention to each other – Which suit did your partner wear last night? Did you notice her new haircut? If you find it hard to answer these questions, it is time to ring the alarm bell. We stop noticing these things when we don't care much about them. Weren't things different when you dated?

You stop taking care of yourself – You may not realize it, but it hurts your partner when you look lackluster.

It shows a lack of love and care if we are always in our pajamas or don't dress up when going out together.

What to do if your relationship has lost the spark?
Get back the spark. It's easy saying, we know, but we can always try and do things differently to get back the relationship on track. Firstly, find out the reasons that made the relationship hit so low. Then, we can think of mending our way up.

Sit and talk – Open communication is the first prerogative for a strong and happy relationship. So, find some free time to converse with your partner. Be frank about your feelings and be ready for some harsh truths. You may not know how your behavior has hurt your mate.

Plan something unique – Do something weird, inimitable, or fun together. Maybe you can go for a safari, join a music class, or learn baking. Start a new hobby like gardening or carpentry so that you can spend time together.

Relive the past – What did you love doing when you were dating? Watching movies or walking in the city? Relive your romance by doing that again. Visit the restaurant where you went for your first date. Watch the movie again that once made both of you cry. These small things will bring back the spark in your love life.

Get out of your comfort zone – We don't realize how we fall into a routine and then complain about boring life. If you want your life to be exciting, get out of your comfort zone and do things differently. Go for a long walk after dinner. Instead of ordering food on weekends, try cooking together. Try a new hairstyle or join the gym.

Go on a date – Yes, this is our favorite suggestion. Plan a date, spend time getting ready, and surprise your partner. Do silly things together, sing or dance like teenagers and have fun.

Revive your sex life – ever tried role-playing? Do it now. Please remember that intimacy is more important than sex. So, cuddle together, kiss passionately, give a massage to your partner, and make the time spent together memorable.

Imagine investing in an NBA player who is the best one on the team. How will you feel if you find his stats decreasing by 20% next year and another 30% in the third year? The same applies to your relationship. Don't let the stats fall.

A relationship is like a plant; water it every day and take care of it to make it bloom. Do things that your partner will value, keep the chase hot, and you will never feel bored.

Conclusion

Wahoo! We have almost reached the end. Thank you for being with me on this fantastic journey. I have enjoyed writing this book so much and poured my heart into it. I have shared my years of experience and observation in planning it to give you the maximum benefit.

As you must have observed, although the book is about attracting women and maintaining relationships, I have gone beyond this and included topics that relate to different aspects of life.

As someone said, "life is 10% what happens to you and 90% how you react to it", so it all begins with the choices we make in life. That's why throughout this book, I have stressed the importance of taking the right decisions at the right time.

When you listen to your heart and take the right path in your life, you enjoy the expedition. Of course, there will be obstacles, and you have to overcome them. This will bolster your confidence and make you stronger.

In this regard, I want to tell you about another vital thing that stops us from realizing our dreams – FEARS.

Didn't you have any friends in college who were afraid of talking to girls? Even smart and confident guys often faltered in front of women. Did you ever wonder what made them so shy? Maybe they feared rejection. But what made them fear rejection? Past experience. Why should your previous experience determine your future?

Here comes the point I wanted to discuss. Most of us are scared of taking a path because we are afraid of failure. This is what stops us from leading the life of our dreams. This is what stops you from talking to that gorgeous girl you met in the library.

Whenever fear grips you, do a little self-talking. Ask yourself what you are afraid of. If you let the fear win over you, what will you lose in life? If you really really want something, nothing can stop you. You just need the courage to go after it.

So, you have to ask yourself what you want and give your best to achieve it. To boost your confidence and increase self-awareness, nothing works better than meditation. That's why I have mentioned it elaborately in this ebook. Once you learn how to meditate and do it daily, you will find your life becoming more beautiful.

Your thoughts will become positive and serene, you will gain clarity and focus better on your goals.

So, follow the tasks I have mentioned in the previous chapters and discover a new you.

Like everything else, when you look for a partner, you have to first decide what you are seeking in her. If you set your priorities first, you will increase your chance of success and also avoid heartbreaks.

If you frequently suffer from anxiety and stress, there is a simple way to avoid these. If you observe your thought patterns you will find out that some specific thoughts trigger anxiety. When you sit for meditation and those thoughts visit your mind, gently set them aside. It will be tough initially as they continue to invade your mind, but with practice, you will be able to replace them with good and positive thoughts. Slowly, this will become a habit and the moment negative thoughts appear in your consciousness, your mind will signal you to switch them to positive ones.

With time, this practice will make you calm and happy. And as everybody knows, a happy person looks attractive. Yes, we are attracted to happy and calm people. We find solace in the company of people who give out positive vibes. Even girls like these guys as they can become frank and talk freely with them.

I want to mention another thing here. At the end of some chapters, I have given a few tasks. You must complete them before moving on. This is essential to use the knowledge you have gained from the book. Unless you put the knowledge to practical use, you cannot reap its benefits. So, make sure that you complete the tasks. If you find any job tough, please go back, read the chapter again, and then attempt the task again.

For difficult tasks, I would suggest jotting them down in a journal and brainstorming ideas that will make it easier for you. This brings us to another important tool of self-development – journaling.

Journaling

When I decided to work on my personality and become a better version of myself, I started reading biographies of great leaders. I came to know about journaling and its benefits. I also took it up and have immensely benefited from it.

So, I will urge all of you to take up journaling and jot down your goals, action plans, and achievements in it. Journaling is a great tool to channel your thoughts, focus on your goals, and solve problems that you face.

For example, you can write down in your journal the qualities you want in your partner and why they are important to you. As you converse with different girls and get to know them, chart down your progress.

This way, your journal will show you where you are getting wrong or what you need to pay attention to.

There is another issue that I must mention here. What will do you if you are trapped in a bad relationship? Firstly, don't blame yourself for getting into a toxic relationship. You made a mistake and it is not a crime. We misjudge people; it's absolutely normal.

When you are stuck in a toxic relationship, you have to decide whether you will continue in it or quit. Decide after thoroughly reviewing the situation as your happiness depends on it.

This book is meant to be a guide that you can follow in your quest for a life partner. However, you can use the tips and ideas to solve problems you face in daily life. I hope this will help you to become happier, more confident, and a successful person.

"You have to work everyday at being the best you can be. It's a project that is never-ending."
~ J. Junior Reynolds II

Lightning Source UK Ltd.
Milton Keynes UK
UKHW010500090223
416681UK00008B/2249